MURDER BY METEORITE

MURDER BY METEORITE

A PLAY IN THREE ACTS

by

WILLIAM MALTESE

THE BORGO PRESS

An Imprint of Wildside Press LLC

MMIX

www.wildsidepress.com

FIRST EDITION

CONTENTS

Illustrations

CAST OF CHARACTERS
in order of appearance

Total: 11

Breakdown by gender:
Female: 3
Male: 8

MELISSA JORDAN
Scrimshaw artist and owner of "Melissa Jordan Galleries" which sell her work, plus the work of other artists. She's the romantic interest of Christian Waynard (See Below).

CAROL WESTINGHAM
Manager of "Melissa Jordan Galleries". During course of the play, her romantic interest becomes John Feaswell

(See Below).

KEVIN SILNER
Artist whose filigree-bone jewelry is handled by the Melissa Jordan Galleries. He learned his skills of filigree while three years as prisoner of war, during his military service in Iraq. His history includes post-traumatic syndrome and extensive hospitalization after his return home and discharge, plus a continuing drug abuse.

ELIZABETH HOWARD
Scientist: astro-geologist. U.S.-government financed and affiliated. Her research involves analysis of meteorites. Personally oversees collection of meteorites "in the field".

COLONEL GREG SAMPSON
Spit-and-polish liaison between Army and Elizabeth Howard (See Above). His history includes term of duty, command capacity, in Iraq.

"ORDERLY"
Iraqi-War vet with ongoing history of drug abuse. "Army-Raider" tattoo on right forearm.

DOCTOR JOHN FEASWELL

Physician, qualified general practitioner, with one-time specialization in plastic surgery. Presently, he's in an administrative capacity at clinic founded by him and named after him. He's a fraternity brother of Christian Waynard (See Below). During the course of the play, his romantic interest becomes Carol Westingham (See Above).

CHRISTIAN WAYNARD

Independently wealthy, with educational background in aquaculture. He's a successful sculptor and interested in making a knife using the iron from a meteorite. He's a fraternity brother of John Feaswell (See Above). He's the romantic interest of Melissa Jordan (See Above).

MAN IN SKI MASK

Iraqi-War vet.

INSPECTOR DWIGHTON

Inspector for the local police department.

LENNY SLINT

Iraqi-War vet and ongoing drug abuser.

TRANSITION to ACT I, Scene 1

House lights dim

LOUD CRASH—of helicopter

Curtain opens on…

ACT I, Scene 1

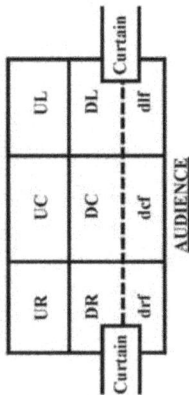

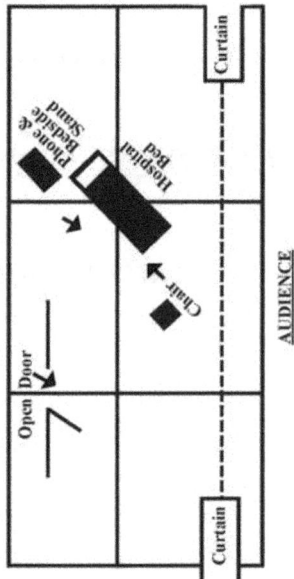

ACT I, Scene 1

room "A"—Feaswell Clinic
open doorway
bedside stand
land-line phone on bedside stand
hospital bed
chair

(MELISSA JORDAN sits up in bed, head UL)

(CAROL WESTINGHAM stands at bedside UC)

(KEVIN SILNER stands, disheveled, at bedside UC, to right of Carol)

MELISSA JORDAN: After five days unconscious, I continue to sleep at the drop of a hat. John says, "There's sleep, then there's sleep." Of course, Christian was discharged two days ago.

(to Kevin) Kevin, I'll understand if you want to cut your visit short.

KEVIN SILNER: (not sounding fine) I'm fine.

MELISSA: John says when the body is subjected to too much stress, the brain overloads and shuts down. Self-repair can take hours, days, sometimes even…. (she shrugs)

CAROL WESTINGHAM: Be sure to take all the time *you* need. I'll hold down the fort.

MELISSA: (to Kevin) Carol keeping you busy, Kevin?

KEVIN: (fishing his pants pocket) I brought you a get-well gift.

(Kevin produces a crumpled cloth that unfolds to reveal the bone-filigree necklace he hands to Melissa)

MELISSA: Kevin, it's beautiful!

CAROL: He insisted he bring it, despite his aversion to hospitals.

MELISSA: That only makes it more special. (she turns the necklace in her fingers)

CAROL: We should head out. Karen Timms is bringing in her carvings. She asked after you. Most of your artists and regulars have. They're waiting to hear if and when you're up to a flood of visitors.

(Carol and Kevin prepare to leave, drifting across UC toward open door)

MELISSA: (calling after) I have hopes of being out of here faster than Doctor John Feaswell probably predicts.

KEVIN: (turning back and nervous) Melissa?

MELISSA: (curiously) Kevin?

KEVIN: (a nervous glance in Carol's direction) Get well.

(Kevin and Carol exit)

(Moments later, Kevin returns through open door and across UC to Melissa's bedside)

KEVIN: I told Carol I'd left my cigarettes. I really wanted to tell you about Captain "Alien". I saw him. He saw me. You and I have to talk about what it all means.

MELISSA: (confused) Kevin, I….

(Enter an armed—with holstered hand gun—U.S. ARMY COLONEL GREG SAMPSON; ELIZABETH HOWARD, on his left)

(Kevin hurriedly exits and almost knocks down the new arrivals)

(ELIZABETH and COLONEL proceed to Melissa's bedside, right of bedside stand; the Colonel closer to foot of bed)

MELISSA: (apologetically) Kevin isn't fond of hospitals.

ELIZABETH HOWARD: (put out but willing to change

subject) I've brought Colonel Greg Sampson, U.S. Army.

MELISSA: We crashed your helicopter, Colonel Sampson.

ARMY COLONEL, GREG SAMPSON: Actually, it was the property of the U.S. taxpayers. I merely arranged for its use: liaison.

MELISSA: There's very little I can tell you, or the American taxpayers. It crashed, washed down a river and over a waterfall. One minute, in the sky; the next ... (palms uplifted)

COLONEL: We sent in a team that would have been on-site sooner with the cooperation of your friend, Christian Waynard.

MELISSA: Oh?

ELIZABETH: As soon as you and Christian were rescued, he, too, under John Feaswell's personal care, Feaswell insisted Christian was medically unfit to see anyone for three days.

COLONEL: Christian unavailable, you comatose, there was no locating your crash site. Before your rescue, you had covered a surprisingly good distance on foot; the wreckage was scattered and not readily observable from the air; and the weather stayed frustratingly erratic. Only after Dr. Feaswell allowed access to Christian did we pinpoint the crash site.

MELISSA: The problem?

COLONEL: Christian has suddenly obtained a meteorite that a Mr. Candive in Nova Scotia just happened to pick up when it dropped from the sky in 1922. Apparently, the stony-iron meteorite has just been waiting all this time for Christian's fat pocketbook.

ELIZABETH: We know what's made from iron. Steel. From steel? A knife blade. That's exactly what Christian told the press he proposes to do with it. Surprised?

MELISSA: Certainly not by what he plans to do with it. Are you? As for this Nova Scotia meteorite, my father picked up two meteorites in 1954 and held onto them until Christian's father showed up with his fat pocketbook, twenty-five years later, didn't he? All the new publicity probably clued in this Mr. Candive, in Nova Scotia, what a jackpot he had.

ELIZABETH: Your attraction to Christian taints your judgment in his favor, my dear.

MELISSA: If I were that attracted, wouldn't I have been acting as *his* guide of the area, instead of yours?

ELIZABETH: I suspect that our luck was in that Christian didn't ask you first.

COLONEL: Elizabeth is concerned that Christian has bilked us of our property.

MELISSA: "Our"? Yours? Elizabeth's? The U.S. government's?

COLONEL: It boils down to what's fair, Melissa.

MELISSA: What's unfair about Mr. Candive selling Christian a rock that's been in his Nova Scotia backyard for years?

COLONEL: Maybe if we mention we've been unable to

locate *our* meteorite at the crash site.

MELISSA: Your meteorite could have broken up in the crash and been washed miles from the scene, as were Christian and I.

ELIZABETH: Someone was there after you but before our team arrived. Someone during the days Christian and you were indisposed and under Dr. John Feaswell's care.

MELISSA: How do you know that?

COLONEL: An on-scene discarded breath-mint wrapper, for one—unless you washed up on one side of the falls, ate your breath mint, discarded its wrapper, re-entered the water, and swam to the opposite shore: an Herculean feat, Melissa, for you or for Christian.

MELISSA: Poachers? Campers? Hikers? One or all hungry, or with bad breath?

COLONEL: We're not "officially" accusing Christian.

ELIZABETH: What do you mean, we're not....

(brought up short by the Colonel's get-it-together stare)

COLONEL: We don't mind losing fairly and merely hope to ascertain whether or not Christian is a cheat.

MELISSA: All of this is between you, Christian, and the U.S. government.

COLONEL: What about your personal efforts on our be-half? All the time you graciously spent as guide to track down the meteorite on land once owned by your father? Do you feel cheated in having won the game, Christian maybe getting the prize?

ELIZABETH: We only want you to persuade Christian to let you take a close look at this conveniently-arrived Nova Scotia meteorite.

MELISSA: Why don't *you* ask him to see it?

ELIZABETH: We have.

COLONEL: Christian is less than cooperative.

MELISSA: Isn't he required to cooperate?

COLONEL: Required?

MELISSA: By the U.S. government.

COLONEL: Christian is wealthy, influential, well-respected. No one wants to call undue attention to U.S. government involvement. Publicity is detrimental to our preferred low profile.

MELISSA: Why *preferred*?

COLONEL: (avoiding the insinuation) If he won't show you, and he won't show us, we'll have to surmise the why.

(BEDSIDE LAND-PHONE RINGS)

(Melissa answers the phone and hands it to Elizabeth)

MELISSA: (to Elizabeth) For you.

(Phone conversation is short, muted, and unintelligible)

(Finished with the call, Elizabeth hands the phone off to Melissa who hangs it up).

ELIZABETH: Seems our helicopter came down, because someone took pains to see it die in the sky.

COLONEL: (not a question) Sabotage.

MELISSA: You're not insinuating Christian, to get his hands on your meteorite, planted a bomb on board before he *then* blasély hitched a ride?

ELIZABETH: Shrapnel pattern and powder burns on the pilot's body....

MELISSA: We buried Captain Miller.

ELIZABETH: Captain Miller was exhumed. Found killed not by impact but by explosion before any of you reached the ground. The bombs were specifically placed to take out the pilot and engine capabilities, sparing the meteorite and *one* specific hitchhiker. Sparing *you*, I would guess, by pure mistake.

MELISSA: You can't find your meteorite, but you can find conclusive evidence of exploded bombs? It was purely luck we survived that drop. Christian wouldn't have risked his life, my life, and ended up killing Captain Miller, for a piece of stone. Not by coming down blind in that rugged terrain, in that wretched weather.

ELIZABETH: He lived! You lived! The pilot didn't die from the fall. The meteorite survived. Christian has it. It's mine.

MELISSA: (disbelieving) All for a chunk of stone? So he can make a knife blade?

COLONEL: So it would seem.

MELISSA: When did Christian plant these bombs? He was with me every second after having gotten Elizabeth's permission to hitch the ride. To have hired someone earlier doesn't seem practical; how could he know there wasn't going to be more survivors to keep him from walking off with the prize? All of our team *could* have been on board.

ELIZABETH: Anyone who so skillfully killed the pilot could as easily have eliminated however many survivors.

MELISSA: He didn't eliminate me!

ELIZABETH: With you, he could afford to play hero. In your condition, you weren't going to give any directions to the crash site. He correctly figured he had plenty of time to send in an extraction crew, especially with his doctor friend's help.

COLONEL: Can you see this compulsion of Christian to follow in his father's knife-making footsteps as less than normal, considering how his father died?

MELISSA: If your father died in a plane crash, would you never fly again?

COLONEL: We do Christian and us a disservice by not setting our suspicious to rest.

(Enter "ORDERLY" with machine-gun concealed under clinic smock. "Orderly" pulls out gun)

(Reflex action propels Melissa out of her bed on the side DL opposite the gunman, pulling her bed blankets with her)

(The Colonel ducks and dives for concealment behind chair DC, simultaneously drawing his pistol and firing as the gunman begins to spray the room with gunfire)

(Elizabeth attempts to go over the bed to join Melissa, but she dies on the bed in the barrage)

("Orderly" goes down, killed by Colonel)

(Lights out)

TRANSITION to ACT I, Scene 2

No close of curtain, during change of props and exit of all characters from stage

Lights up on ...

ACT I, Scene 2

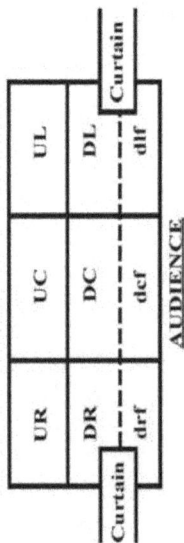

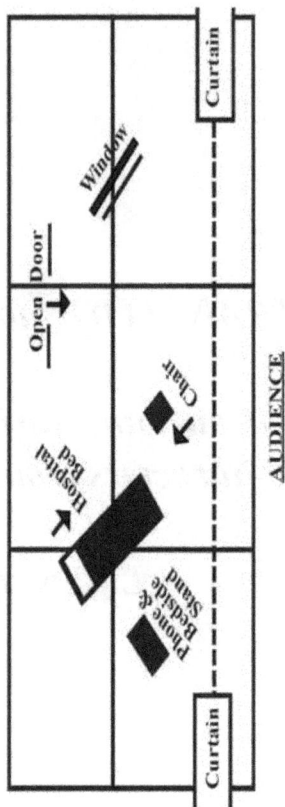

ACT I, Scene 2

room "B" Feaswell Clinic:
open doorway
bedside stand
phone on bedside stand
hospital bed
chair
window

(Melissa and DOCTOR JOHN FEASWELL enter via door; Melissa is wrapped in bed clothes and supported by John)

(Melissa and John proceed to bed where John eases Melissa onto bed)

(Enter CHRISTIAN WAYNARD, via door, in state of extreme agitation)

MELISSA: (spotting Christian) Christian!

(Christian Waynard rushes to bed; he greets Melissa with a hug)

CHRISTIAN WAYNARD: (to John) My God, John, is Melissa all right? I hear Elizabeth Howard is dead.

MELISSA: (distraught) Elizabeth dead?

JOHN FEASWELL: (consoling Melissa) Let's worry about you.

(to Christian) If I can believe in miracles, Melissa came through with only scratches. Bruises will show later.

MELISSA: The Colonel?

CHRISTIAN: Arm wound for Billy-the-kid Colonel who out-gunned the bastard-with-the-real-fire-power. John is going to have to hire himself a new orderly, though.

JOHN: Except, the dead shooter isn't one of mine. I know all the vets on my staff.

MELISSA: Vet?

JOHN: "Army Raider" tattoo on his right forearm.

CHRISTIAN: He came gunning for the Colonel, then?

JOHN: I'm a medical doctor, old buddy. You want motivation, you need a psychiatrist or police investigator. You'll have the latter shortly. Why don't I fetch a sedative to give Melissa a good night's rest before the bombardment of questions?

MELISSA: I'm the last person with answers.

JOHN: That won't stop the police from asking.

(John exits to door)

CHRISTIAN: (to Melissa) This isn't how I planned our reunion.

MELISSA: As good a time as any to thank you for literally hauling me out of the wilderness on your back.

CHRISTIAN: (with accompanying quick kiss) My pleasure.

(Enter John with syringe; he crosses to bed and administers the injection into Melissa's arm; he exits back through door)

(Melissa settles down on the bed; Christian sooths her brow)

CHRISTIAN: We'll play catch-up tomorrow.

MELISSA: No reflection on your frat buddy's clinic, but I want out of it.

CHRISTIAN: We can talk about that tomorrow, too.

(Melissa lifts to wrap Christian's neck and give him a swift kiss)

(Fade to black)

TRANSITION to ACT I, Scene 3

No close of curtain

In darkness, Christian exits, and John enters and positions himself at window in its UL/DL diagonal

Lights go up fast to coincide with John pulling curtains of window to reveal a new day and...

ACT I, Scene 3

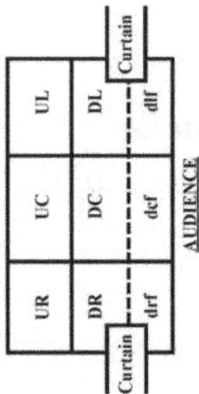

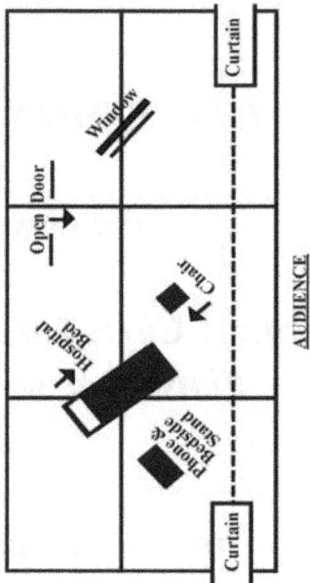

ACT I, Scene 3
(same as ACT I, Scene 2)

(John at window)

(Melissa revives in bed; she's lethargic in the aftermath of the sedative)

MELISSA: John, can you tell me Colonel Sampson's room number?

JOHN: Colonel Sampson transferred to an Army medical facility.

MELISSA: He is all right, though?

JOHN: He was bitching about his arm cast, but considering everything…yeah…I'd say he's all right.

MELISSA: I'm checking out, too. Immediately after breakfast.

JOHN: Oh? No longer sure Carol can manage your business affairs, are you?

MELISSA: I didn't say that.

(John crosses to bed)

JOHN: Carol looked eminently competent when I saw her in your downtown gallery. I was after something special for an old friend, and Christian assured me nothing was more special than one of your scrimshaw pieces. Carol sold me a marvelous walrus tusk—"The Marimet Rounding Cape Horn."

MELISSA: I'm surprised she didn't mention meeting you.

JOHN: I thought she might take my name-dropping as hint for a discount.

MELISSA: Thereby giving me an opening to bargain Clinic rates?

JOHN: Haven't I told you: your treatment and Christian's are on the house? I owe him.

MELISSA: How hard I argue depends on my insurance. In the meantime, I'll tell Carol you get double discount on anything else that catches your fancy.

JOHN: Could you tell her by noon today?

MELISSA: There's another piece you like?

JOHN: Something other than Carol, you mean?

MELISSA: (reluctant) I hate to be the one to …

JOHN: (interrupting) Carol and I are having lunch. I promise my best behavior.

MELISSA: (surprised) You and Carol? Lunch?

JOHN: To discuss, among other things, that second piece of I-have-to-have scrimshaw.

MELISSA: Then, how quickly I get to her about your double discount depends only upon how quickly you can check me out of here.

JOHN: It may surprise you that I'm a firm believer that people mend faster out of hospitals than in them. If you're up to it, I see no reason why you shouldn't be home as soon as you're steady on your feet. Take a few steps this morning, and I'll check back about noon. We can aim for a two-thirty release if all goes well.

MELISSA: (disbelieving) You're serious?

JOHN: Cross my heart. (belatedly, he does so)

(John moves toward door but brings himself up short and turns back toward Melissa on the bed)

JOHN: Before you're out of here, you should probably know that I'm the one, not Christian, responsible for the clandestine team sent in to recover Elizabeth Howard's lost meteorite.

MELISSA: You?!

JOHN: Elizabeth and the Colonel blame Christian, right?

MELISSA: Good guess!

JOHN: Truth is, I knew how badly Christian wanted that rock, and I knew where it was supposed to be, because I asked Christian when you both checked in. I sent a team in. Unfortunately, it came back with zilch.

MELISSA: Meaning, this meteorite Christian ends up with *is* a different one that *really* did come down in Nova Scotia years ago?

JOHN: Cross my heart. (belatedly, he does so)

MELISSA: But when Elizabeth asked to see it, Christian refused.

JOHN: It had to do with the way she asked, all foaming at the mouth in front of reporters.

MELISSA: If Elizabeth had been allowed to look, she would have realized her mistake and quit making a fuss. Christian wasn't playing fair.

JOHN: Maybe, but don't hold it against him, will you?

(prepares to leave) Remember what I said about testing your sea legs.

(John exits via door)

(Melissa eases herself off bed, DR-side, beside bedside stand)

(BEDSIDE LAND-LINE PHONE RINGS and Melissa answers)

TRANSITION to ACT I, Scene 4

As curtain begins slow close…

Carol, cell phone in hand, her blouse stained in front with bloody tic-tac-toe-like striations, enters in front of curtain, dlf, along with MAN IN SKI MASK who holds knife in the small of Carol's back

CAROL: (into cell phone) Melissa; it's Carol. Any word as to when they let you out?

(Melissa carries her phone, cord stretching the distance, slowly around bottom of bed and toward Stage Center, so that, during the course of the ensuing conversation, the slowly closing curtain provides her with parenthesis)

MELISSA: (into her phone) Would you believe we're aiming for two-thirty this very afternoon?

CAROL: If so, can we meet?

MELISSA: Are you okay?

CAROL: (evasive) You know Denton Park. Could you take a cab? I can drive you home from there. Three o'clock?

MELISSA: Can't you give me a clue?

(Curtain completes closure to conceal Melissa)

(MAN IN SKI MASK takes cell phone from Carol and deactivates it)

MAN IN SKI MASK: Don't think you can change anything.

CAROL: Please.

(Carol collapses to stage)

(Man in Ski Mask exits Stage Left, via dlf, in front of closed curtain)

(Lights fade to lone spotlight on Carol which dissolves to coincide with spotlight isolating Melissa who enters Stage Right, drf—in front of closed curtain)

(Melissa is dressed for the street and wears the filigree necklace given her by Kevin at the hospital)

(Melissa proceeds in front of closed curtain toward Stage Left)

MELISSA: (spotting Carol) Carol?

CAROL: Melissa?

(Carol runs to more slow-moving Melissa; the two meet where closed curtain meets, dcf; Melissa's spotlight expands to include both women who embrace)

(Melissa pulls back and, with hand movements, indicates the bloodstains on Carol's blouse)

MELISSA: My God, what happened?

CAROL: I'm so sorry.

(Man in Ski Mask suddenly appears through slot of closed curtain and grabs Melissa in a choke hold; he drags her deeper into concealed Stage Center as…)

(…Lights go on)

ACT I, Scene 4

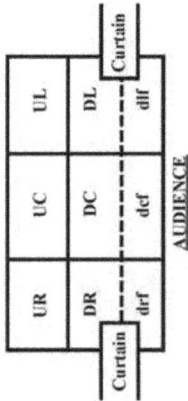

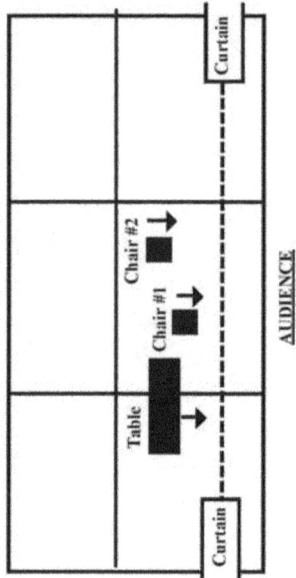

ACT I, Scene 4

interior of Man in Ski Mask hideout
chair #1 with ropes attached to back and legs
chair #2 with ropes attached to back and legs
table—on which is placed:
a briefcase in which there's a cell phone
a billy-club
pair of handcuffs
whip
brass knuckles
sundry other implements of torture

(Man in Ski Mask drops a nearly asphyxiated Melissa into Chair #1; he begins to tie her to Chair #1 with available ropes)

(Carol attacks Man in Ski Mask)

CAROL: (involved in attack on Man in Ski Mask) No! No! No!

(Man in Ski Mask backhands Carol)

(Carol goes down, on collision with table, and she's knocked immediately unconscious as the material on the tabletop is scattered)

(Man in Ski Mask goes back to completing his tie-up of Melissa to Chair #1)

MELISSA: (with just enough breath to speak) What is it you want?

MAN IN SKI MASK: You tell me.

MELISSA: I haven't the foggiest.

MAN IN SKI MASK: This time, you're dealing with me, not with that incompetent doper Clamer.

MELISSA: Clamer?

MAN IN SKI MASK: The magician who fired bullets into a roomful of people but only killed one. Want to tell me how he managed that?

MELISSA: The Iraqi-War vet, masquerading as a Clinic orderly, who had something against Colonel Sampson?

MAN IN SKI MASK: It's my understanding he killed Elizabeth Howard, only wounding Colonel Sampson. Thereby, you, his intended victim got off scot-free. Unless you've bullet holes I don't see.

MELISSA: (aghast) Why would he kill me?

MAN IN SKI MASK: Why would I kidnap you? Something to do with Kevin Silner, do you suppose?

MELISSA: With Kevin?

MAN IN SKI MASK: You do know him? Army vet and basket-case. Artist. You're wearing one of his pieces, if I'm not mistaken. (he fingers filigree necklace around Melissa's neck)

(The CELL PHONE IN BRIEFCASE RINGS, muffled by

briefcase now knocked—either to a new position on the table or onto the floor)

(Man in Ski Mask proceeds to briefcase, opens it, and retrieves ringing phone; simultaneously, a revived Carol retrieves the billy-club—or handcuffs, or brass knuckles, or...—from where it landed and springs on Man in Ski Mask, smashing him a glancing blow on the head)

(Man in Ski Masks goes down in obvious pain)

(Carol rushes to Melissa and begins untying Melissa)

CAROL: A nightmare!

(The revived-but-reeling Man in Ski Mask yanks Carol away from Melissa and sends Carol sprawling)

(Melissa fights the efforts of Man in Ski Mask to refasten the bonds on Melissa that Carol has unfastened)

(Carol recovers and returns to the fray, jumps on the back of Man in Ski Mask)

(Man in Ski Mask dislodges Carol while Melissa successfully frees herself completely of the ropes, gets up, picks up a billy-club—or handcuffs, or brass knuckles, or…—and whacks Man in Ski Mask)

(Man in Ski Mask goes down)

(Curtain begins to close as Melissa goes to give Carol a helping hand)

MELISSA: Come on, Carol! Come on!

(Melissa and Carol attempt to flee through the narrowing breach of closing curtain, but Man in Ski Mask grabs Carol's leg)

(A free-for-all results as curtain completes its close, con-cealing the still-struggling trio)

(Melissa and Carol, shrieking in peril, exit through breach of closed curtain and run off Stag Right, via drf, in front of closed curtain)

(End of ACT I)

(House lights on)

TRANSITION to ACT II, Scene 1

House lights dim to black

Curtain remains closed

Spotlight isolates Melissa and Carol warily entering from Stage Right, drf, in front of closed curtain, in progress toward center dcf, in front of closed curtain

CAROL: What if he comes back?

MELISSA: You have a better idea? It could be miles to the nearest phone. On the other hand, we both saw him leave without his cell phone, didn't we?

CAROL: And if that's what he plans for us to think? He didn't exactly sneak off.

MELISSA: You hide here. He can't be two places at once. If he comes back and catches me, *you* make the long trek, wherever, for help; I'll take my chances.

CAROL: I should be the one to go back in. I got you into this.

MELISSA: I've no energy for a long hike. The good doctor was fighting to hold me an extra day. Speaking of Dr. John Feaswell, I understand you and he are "an item", these days.

(she doesn't wait for a response) Get down—

(she motions toward the curtain folds)—over there and wait. I'll try to make this fast.

(Melissa disappears through center slit of closed curtain)

(Carol hunkers down in an attempt to conceal herself within closed curtain folds)

(Spotlight fades, then brightens as Melissa returns back dcf, in front of closed curtain through center slit of closed curtain; she has the retrieved cell phone in hand)

(Carol rises from "hiding")

MELISSA: Confident bastard didn't even break it. I called John to tend to whatever that sicko did to cause all that blood on your blouse. Besides, John can use his clout to make sure the cops sit up and take notice.

(she doesn't wait for any response) Come on, let's fade more into the landscape until our White Knight arrives.

(Melissa and Carol slowly proceed back into drf, the way they've entered, in front of curtain)

(The two stop in drf)

MELISSA: Needless to say, John was surprised to hear the real reason you canceled your lunch date. It was a date, right? First one I can remember you having, since you turned up on my doorstep with Kevin. So, where does that put Kevin as the steady in your life? Other than in deep shit if he's responsible for any or all of this?

CAROL: Kevin's my brother, not my steady, Melissa.

MELISSA: (obviously caught off-guard) Wha'?!

CAROL: We thought you'd guessed.

MELISSA: (incredulously) Right! Kevin *Silner*. Carol *Westingham*. We're talking some pretty esoteric clues.

CAROL: Blame Gregory Westingham.

MELISSA: Full of surprises; you have a husband, too?

CAROL: For two months when I was sixteen, he twenty. Disastrous. Horrible. Not something I talk about.

MELISSA: Obviously. Maiden name: Silner?

CAROL: Maiden name: Templin.

MELISSA: How silly of me not to have known that.

CAROL: Silner is the identity Kevin assumed when he bolted the VA hospital. It took me six years to find him, and he only recognizes me part time. The shrinks say he's running from himself. They haven't a clue as to why, except, "The war screwed up a lot of peoples' heads."

(Carol and Melissa sit drf in front of closed curtain)

CAROL: When I was a kid, Kevin was fun and full of life. He came back from Iraq a drained, broken, shell of a man. Three years a prisoner of war. Eleven months in turkey pens where thousands of birds had been machine-gunned by retreating forces with a Sherman-march-too-the-sea mentality.

(pause) There was this local artisan accused of collaboration. The Iraqi broke all of this guy's fingers, then his arms. He kept an awl hidden, but not to kill himself. He'd grip the awl with the toes of one foot to punch filigree into turkey bones he'd hold with the toes of his other foot. "Beauty is where you choose to find it," he told Kevin, "even in a boneyard of soon-too-die men and long-dead fowl." (she sobs)

(FAST-MOVING AUTO BRAKES TO A STOP off dlf, stage left)

(Spotlight extinguishes and is immediately replaced by auto headlights originating off dlf, Stage Left, and illuminating the crouching Melissa and Carol, drf, in front of closed curtain. The women are as blinded and as hypnotized as any two deer caught in a poacher's illegal spotlight)

(Melissa and Carol get up and bolt off Stage Right)

CHRISTIAN: (from off Stage Left) Melissa?

(Stage Left, Christian steps into headlight beams and onto stage, dlf, in front of closed curtain, followed by John)

JOHN: Carol?

MELISSA: (from off Stage Right) Christian, is that you?

JOHN: Me, too!

(Melissa and Carol rush from Stage Right, via drf, via dcf, to dlf and the two men. Melissa and Christian automatically fall into each other's arms. Carol and John greet with more caution, although they, too, conclude with an, albeit gentle, hug)

(Carol sobs)

JOHN: (putting Carol at extended arms'-lengths) Melissa said the bastard cut you.

(Carol's hands automatically flatten across the front of her blood-stained blouse)

CHRISTIAN: More bad news: Kevin Silner has just been found murdered in Melissa's condo.

MELISSA: What?

(Carol faints. John catches her and eases her drop to the stage)

(Melissa and Christian attend collapsed Carol)

MELISSA: Kevin's her brother.

CHRISTIAN: (apologetically) Damn!

MELISSA: Who was to know? I only just found out.

JOHN: (to Melissa) The Clinic has a V.I.P. condo, and we'll check you both in there until we can sort out this mess, including the one in progress at your place.

(John lifts Carol into his arms)

MELISSA: What was Kevin doing at my condo?

CHRISTIAN: Inspector Dwighton is hoping you can tell him.

(Melissa, Christian, and John-carrying-Carol, exit Stage Left)

(Off Stage Left, CAR DOORS OPEN, SHUT.

(Car lights, until then shining onto stage, in front of closed curtain, swerve and disappears as car off-stage "turns")

(Curtain opens on…)

ACT II, Scene 1

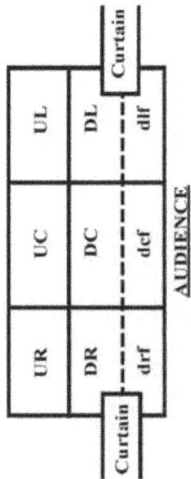

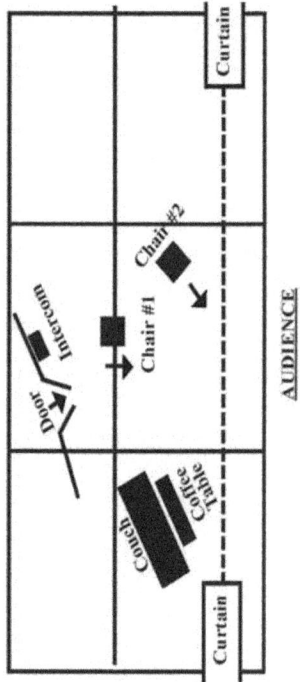

ACT II, Scene 1

interior of V.I.P. condo owned by Feaswell Clinic:
door, able to open and shut
intercom and buzzer, on wall adjoining door
couch
coffee table
chair #1
chair #2

(Carol lies on couch, head toward Stage Right)

(Melissa is seated in chair #1)

(Christian is seated in chair #2)

(John converses on cell phone as he paces DC/DL)

(John finishes his conversation on the cell phone)

JOHN: Apparently, Inspector Dwighton is on his way.

(The INTERCOM BUZZER SOUNDS)

MELISSA: Speak of the Devil.

(Carol sits up on couch, at farthest point Stage Right)

(John goes to intercom)

JOHN: Come in, Inspector.

MELISSA: (to no one in particular) And bring some answers with you.

(Melissa vacates her chair #1 for place on couch, nearest Center Stage)

(KNOCK ON DOOR)

(John lets in INSPECTOR DWIGHTON and leads him

DC)

JOHN: (to Inspector) I think you know everyone, but Carol, from that nastiness at the Clinic.

(Carol raises her hand in greeting)

(The Inspector nods in Carol's direction)

(John indicates Inspector should take chair #1; Inspector sits)

(John sits between Melissa and Carol on couch and puts cell phone on coffee table in front of him)

INSPECTOR: (to Carol) I understand you're the victim's sister.

CAROL: Yes.

INSPECTOR: (removing small notebook from one pocket) What about your wounds?

JOHN: Deep enough for scarring.

INSPECTOR: You're lucky in that he's killed….

MELISSA, CAROL, JOHN, CHRISTIAN: (in unison) Killed?!

INSPECTOR: …three women, possibly four.

MELISSA: Dear God!

JOHN: Why haven't I read anything about it in the papers?

INSPECTOR: Until now, his victims haven't been prominent. Besides which, we purposely chose to downplay the murders because of the sensationalistic aspects of them which could do more harm than good for our investigation.

CAROL: I knew he planned to kill us.

INSPECTOR: We'll need a detailed description.

MELISSA: Ski mask. Cuts women. Beyond that, he was less than obliging.

INSPECTOR: Maybe you'll think of something. Meanwhile, let's see if we can't put rhyme or reason to the death of Kevin Silner.

CAROL: For a long time, now, I've expected my brother to end up like this.

INSPECTOR: Oh?

CAROL: Drugs. You aren't telling me this has nothing to do with them. Buying. Selling. Using. Abusing. He's been high most of the time he's been back from Iraq. Such a waste!

(Carol fishes in her pocket for a handkerchief and dabs her eyes with it)

MELISSA: (to Inspector) Any clues as to why Kevin was at my condo?

INSPECTOR: He told the building super he was there to water your plants. Something, I take it, he's done before.

MELISSA: Once. I went to Europe. Carol broke her ankle. Kevin filled in.

INSPECTOR: There's a disjointed message from him on your answering machine.

CHRISTIAN: He called to let her know he was setting up a drug deal at her place?

INSPECTOR: Maybe he was just confused; the recording suggests he was high at the time. Maybe, he called to make sure she wasn't back from the hospital, her condo empty and convenient.

JOHN: Drugs found on the premises?

INSPECTOR: Several packets of coke: very high-grade: cut only twice. I'm surprised the killer didn't take them, but he might have been short on time. It was the racket that had neighbors call in the complaint.

(he takes out his cell phone, calls up a picture from its pictures file, and gets up; he hands the phone to Melissa; then he assumes a position facing the audience, to peer over Melissa's shoulder) I understand, Melissa, that you're our expert on scrimshaw.

MELISSA: (identifying the picture called up on the cell phone monitor) This is a picture of one of my scrimshaw pieces. "The Neptune Brig on the Rocks at Point Hatteras", last seen on the coffee table in my living room.

INSPECTOR: There's a particular style and technique for every artist? A piece like that wouldn't even have to be signed, and anyone would know it was by you?

MELISSA: If by "anyone" you mean someone who knows artists and scrimshaw.

INSPECTOR: One artist, though, pretty much recognizes the work of the competition? How the scrimshaw is scratched into the matrix, whether a piece depicts a sailing ship, or a horse, whether it's in black ink or in color?

CHRISTIAN: (irritated) This leads somewhere?

INSPECTOR: I can hope.

(The Inspector leans over and calls up another picture on the cell-phone monitor)

MELISSA: (examining the new picture and surprised by what she sees) This second picture is of one of the five knives made by Christian's father, and hilted by mine, over ten years ago. It was one of two made from meteorites found on my father's wilderness property in the fifties. My father sold both meteorites to Christian's father who melted them down for their iron to make steel blades. Both knives became part of Christian's father's private collection.

(The Inspector takes back the cell phone and passes it to Christian)

CHRISTIAN: Melissa's right.

INSPECTOR: (to Christian) A man who collected his own knives? Doesn't one usually collect the works of others?

CHRISTIAN: Many knives, including those made in the collaboration of Melissa's father with mine, are genuine works of art, recognized even by their makers as such.

INSPECTOR: Deadly pieces of art.

MELISSA: Using an ashtray to kill someone doesn't make it less an ashtray.

INSPECTOR: (to Christian) Your father's collection was stolen at the time of his murder, yes? Neither killer nor collection ever found?

CHRISTIAN: Since you have a photo of that particular knife, I assume you know something we don't.

INSPECTOR: That knife killed Kevin Silner. Left so securely lodged within his muscle tissue that the killer couldn't have pulled it free even if he'd wanted.

(Carol gasps)

INSPECTOR: (to Carol) My apologies.

MELISSA: This is all just so bizarre!

CHRISTIAN: More so when you realize this isn't the first knife of that stolen collection used in a murder.

INSPECTOR: I beg your pardon.

CHRISTIAN: You should contact the Los Angeles Police Department and ask for Detective Paolo Sánchez. He was up here a couple of years ago to have me identify a knife connected to the murders of several prostitutes in the L.A. area.

INSPECTOR: Could you be more specific?

CHRISTIAN: The L.A. murder knife was, also, from meteorite.

INSPECTOR: Made from one of those two meteorites down on the property of Melissa's father in the fifties and sold to your father for melt down?

CHRISTIAN: No. It was made from a meteorite down in Baja, Mexico in the twenties.

MELISSA: A killer with a penchant for knives made from meteorites? Who would have guessed?

INSPECTOR: We don't want to make any such hasty conclusion. Imagine the field day the press would have with "E.T. Killer", or "Death Weapons from the Moon". We'd have banner headlines on every supermarket tabloid from here to Timbuktu. Every U.F.O. fanatic within six-thousand miles would tumble out of the woodwork. Besides, how many knives were in that stolen collection, anyway? One-hundred fifty? One-hundred sixty? Why scoop up all that excess when all he wanted was three?

MELISSA: Maybe he didn't want the police or anyone else to see the trees for the forest.

INSPECTOR: More likely, he picked the murder weapons at random from those available to him and came up with the two from meteorite by mere chance.

CHRISTIAN: You want the mathematics that say the odds are against that?

INSPECTOR: The assumption you've both made is that the killer, one day, decided to commit a few murders with only knives made from meteorites, for which purpose he stole three such knives, among a collection of one-hundred-sixty "art" knives. When one meteorite knife got left in a body in L.A., he used meteorite knife two, which he lost in Kevin Silner's body, here. Not to worry; he still has a third meteorite knife in backup, somewhere, for his next killing.

CHRISTIAN: There was a meteorite knife in the Dailinity Collection, one in the Freeburg Collection, one in the Masner Collection: all three of those collections stolen without a trace. Maybe the killer's weapons reserve includes those meteorite knives as well.

INSPECTOR: (threatening) I expect you to keep any such outer-space bullshit nonsense under wraps.

CAROL: These women killed in L.A. were prostitutes?

(she gets up and crosses to Christian)

(to Christian) May I see that photo, please?

(Christian hands over the cell phone to Carol)

CAROL: (distraught) It's the knife that freak in the ski mask used to cut me!

(hysterical) It's the same one, I tell you. The very same!

(Everyone seated gets up to calm Carol; the group effort

finally succeeds)

JOHN: (to Inspector) If it's all right with you, Inspector, I'll take Carol into the other room and give her a sedative.

(John doesn't wait for the Inspector's permission but ushers Carol off Stage Left as the Inspector skillfully retrieves his cell phone from Carol's hand as she passes by; he pockets the phone)

MELISSA: (taking her place back on couch) We could all use sedatives. What are the chances, Inspector, that we can stop now and resume this interview some other time?

INSPECTOR: I really would like to cover a couple more points, here and now, if I could. One of which is the message Kevin left on your answering machine.

(Inspector thumbs through his notebook)

(Christian sits on chair #1)

(Inspector sits in chair #2)

INSPECTOR: (reading from his notebook) "Melissa? Melissa? Melissa? We have to talk. Important. Interesting. Very interesting. Dangerous. Possibly very dangerous. Too dangerous to lay it on Carol. Too dangerous to lay it on you, but I think you should know. I wanted to tell you at the hospital, but the Colonel with the old hag scared the shit out of me. Major heart-attack time. Bad vibes. Sweats. Flashes. Shakes. Want you to understand. Maybe you can figure. I'll come by tonight. Six o'clock."

(he looks up from his notebook) Kevin Silner was dead by six-fifteen.

MELISSA: I've no idea what any of it means.

INSPECTOR: How about someone called Captain Halien?

(another check of his notebook) Kevin's dying words:

(reading from notebook) "Captain Halien forgot we had the same teacher."

MELISSA: (after some thought) "Alien." "Captain Alien." Without any "H."

INSPECTOR: Please tell me we're not back in outer space.

MELISSA: Kevin came back for a few minutes at the Clinic after Carol left, before Elizabeth and Colonel Sampson arrived. He insisted we needed to talk—about "Captain Alien".

INSPECTOR: (dismissively) People on drugs often have visits from aliens, from the Jolly Green Giant, and from the Cabbage That Ate Cleveland; not necessarily in that order.

(John enters from Stage Left; he carries his doctor's bag)

JOHN: As attending physician, I'm going to insist further questions of one and all be postponed until later.

(to Inspector) If your office would call mine, we can coordinate.

(Inspector closes his notebook)

INSPECTOR: This would go faster if we could get it over in one sitting, but…. (he shrugs reluctant acceptance)

JOHN: (not persuaded) Let me show you the door.

(John leads Inspector to door and opens it)

(Neither Melissa nor Christian get up but follow action with their eyes and body shifts)

(Inspector exits)

(John closes the door and leans his back against it)

JOHN: I have to check in at the Clinic to see whatever the inevitable crises arisen during my absence.

(he checks his wristwatch) Anyone for a sedative?

MELISSA: I'll be fine, John, and thanks for everything.

(John exists through the door)

CHRISTIAN: (coming to his feet) My cue to give you some time to yourself.

MELISSA: Before you leave, I'm up to explanations as to how, when, and why you decided to trap the man who killed your father and who now appears to have killed several women here, several more in Los Angeles; not to mention having used Carol as a carving board and, likely, killed Kevin.

CHRISTIAN: I.... (pauses on his own initiative)

MELISSA: I've guessed what you're up to with this Nova Scotia meteorite, Christian. I doubt you can convince me otherwise.

CHRISTIAN: Maybe if I put it in perspective, then?

MELISSA: Feel free to give it a try.

CHRISTIAN: (pacing) One of my first memories of my father is him home from a hard day at the office, relaxing in the shed out back by stoking up the forge and beating on a piece of heated metal.

He would have been a blacksmith in some other

time.

He would have been a blacksmith in his time if it hadn't been for his father insisting he be "more".

So, Dad ended up with the big money, the big office, the big house, the big car. But, in his opinion, he never had it all until his father died, and Dad remodeled one of the out-buildings at our country place and moved in a genuine blacksmith from Lillooet who stayed on to teach Dad every nuance of banging steel.

I'd sneak in to watch amid all those sounds of ringing metal. That shed was an alchemist's lair, more so than the stereotype with beakers, test tubes, mortars, and pestles. Gleaming knife blades emerged from drab ingots, like streamlined butterflies from chunky cocoons.

I wanted to perform that kind of magic, but, at first, I was too young. Then, I had to learn the basics that seldom produced anything exciting. By the time I did get the fundamentals down, I was bored and detoured to other interests: cars, women, sports, school, aquaculture, sculpture; not necessarily in that order.

Suddenly, it was Dad forever asking, "Make that knife today, will we, Christian?", while I was off to do something else.

MELISSA: (perceptively) A knife never made, then, by the two of you—together—as father and son.

(Christian sits in Chair #1)

CHRISTIAN: A freelance writer came around awhile back to interview me for an article for "Blade" magazine. Subject: great knives stolen over the last few years. The Jilian dagger, with the Kerton emerald in its hilt; the Samiston dirk out of that fancy platinum alloy. A couple of Dad's knives. This guy had inventories of the stolen collections.

MELISSA: Which allowed you to notice how several thieves had, between them, a good deal of all meteorite knives, or one thief had the whole enchilada.

CHRISTIAN: About the same time, Detective Sánchez showed from L.A., and I realized I was out to nab a psychopath. Nonetheless, I finally knew meteorite knives were what this freak was all about.

MELISSA: You don't think you'd be better off with the police in on this with you? All outward appearances tell me Inspector Dwighton doesn't have a clue as to what you're up to.

CHRISTIAN: The police have had all the chances I'm willing to give them. Having the murder weapon in L.A. didn't get results. This second murder weapon isn't going to do them any better—you wait and see. You heard Inspector Dwighton's paranoia about the press accusing him of chasing some outer-space killer.

(Christian's CELL PHONE RINGS)

(He takes his ringing cell phone from his pocket and answers it)

CHRISTIAN: (into cell phone) Yes?

(curiously, handing the cell phone over to Melissa) It's for you.

TRANSITION to ACT II, Scene 2

Curtain begins slow close as ...

In front of closing curtain, dlf, LENNY SLINT enters; he wears a large-pocket jacket and has a cell phone which his hand has at his ear; he drags a kitchen chair behind him, en route to center dcf, in front of curtain; the curtain, closing, keeps in time with Lenny's progress.

LENNY: Melissa Jordan?

(Melissa's response isn't heard)

(As Lenny reaches center dcf, still in front of closing curtain, the curtain completes full closure)

LENNY: (into cell phone) You don't know me, Melissa, but Kevin Silner and I were fellow Army vets. Most recently, we met up in a local bar, "VN Sally's". There for alcohol and…other recreational activities. Something occurred there that Kevin thought you might find of interest. Did he ever get around to telling you?

(pause) Never mind how I knew to call you on Christian Waynard's phone. I have my sources. Just answer my question, please.

(pause) I thought maybe Kevin might have told you, seeing as there was all that gunfire at the Clinic. "Army Raider" tattoo on the gunman's right forearm, yes?

(pause) Someone, that same description, complete with money-filled pockets, tried to ax me the day before the Clinic shooting. I was too faster for him, though. Last I saw of him, he still had his tattoo, but his pockets were decidedly emptier than when I cold-cocked him.

(pause as Lenny positions the kitchen chair so its back is to the audience; he straddles the chair, facing the audience, his arms propped on back of chair as he continues talking into the phone) I don't think telling you over the phone is necessarily a good idea.

(pause) Inspector Dwighton happen to mention to you that Kevin's phone was bugged?

(pause) Well, I don't suppose he figured you had need-to-know. He certainly wouldn't figure *I* had need-to-know, but I know someone who knows someone who knows someone who knows Kevin's phone was kinked with some pretty sophisticated shit. Top-grade. *Mucho*-expensive. Government-issue. Inspector Dwighton figures it was bought with drug money. A lot of that floating around these days. Personally, I never found Kevin involved with drug-land's big-moneyed big-boys. So, maybe, there's another explanation?

(pause) You come on down to 1022 N.E. Crescent Boulevard, and we'll discuss at least one other possibility.

(pause) In the front door, turn right, go down the hall, turn left, left again. Wait for me by the elevators. You don't show in fifteen minutes, I'll figure you're not interested.

(in seeming afterthought) Oh, yeah, bring a flashlight but no one else.

(Lenny disconnects and slips the phone into his jacket pocket; he checks his wristwatch, after which he rests his head on his arms, along the back of the chair, and waits)

(Lenny checks his wristwatch again)

MELISSA: (off Stage Left talking to Christian) It has to be this next building.

CHRISTIAN: (off Stage Left talking to Melissa) Except, this is no next building. At least not much of one. It's been gutted by a fire.

(Lenny, taking his chair with him, disappears through joining of closed curtain into concealed DC segment of stage)

(Melissa and Christian enter dlf, in front of closed curtain; Melissa has flashlight, but it's not turned on)

CHRISTIAN: Someone is playing a sick joke.

(Melissa and Christian proceed to center dcf, in front of closed curtain)

(Melissa slightly parts breach in closed curtain and looks

through to concealed DC)

MELISSA: It has a front door. He did say bring a flash-light.

CHRISTIAN: Melissa, this building is condemned: a death trap. I'm not about to let you or me wander inside it, on the off chance there's a madman in there, waiting.

MELISSA: (checking her wristwatch) He did say fifteen minutes.

(Melissa flicks on flashlight and steps through the breach in the closed curtain, disappearing into concealed DC)

CHRISTIAN: (reaching to stop Melissa but not succeed-ing) Melissa!

(Christian follows Melissa through the breach in closed curtains; all lights, with the exception of flashlight, go out as closed curtain opens behind Christian to reveal....)

ACT II, Scene 2

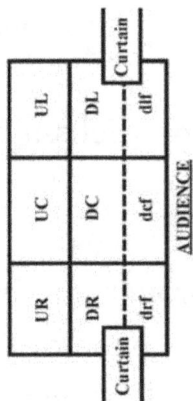

UR	UC	UL
DR	DC	DL
drf	dcf	dlf

AUDIENCE

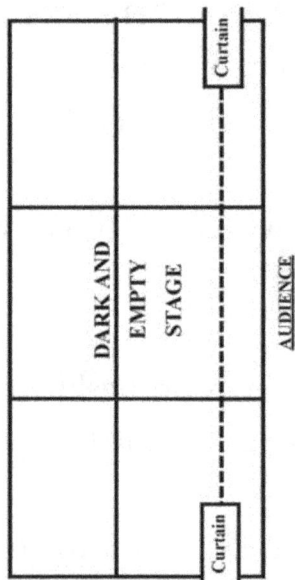

DARK AND
EMPTY
STAGE

AUDIENCE

ACT II, Scene 2

interior fire-gutted building, represented by a completely dark and empty stage.

(Melissa is DL, her flashlight on)

(Christian joins Melissa DL)

CHRISTIAN: (perturbed) We should have brought a gun.

MELISSA: I'm not even sure how Lenny is going to react to my bringing you.

(In dark, Melissa and Christian proceed to edge of Stage Left, make left turn, another left turn, and head back toward Center Stage)

MELISSA: Somewhere, there's an elevator.

CHRISTIAN: (facetiously) Which, I'm sure, works perfectly.

(In dark, Lenny enters from Stage Left and knocks flashlight out of Melissa's hand: flashlight skitters across floor)

(Lenny grabs Melissa and drags her after him to exit Stage Left)

CHRISTIAN: (disoriented, distraught, and going for Melissa's flashlight) Melissa? Damn it! Melissa! That bastard hurts you, I'll kill him.

(Curtain closes)

(End of ACT II)

(House lights up)

TRANSITION to ACT III, Scene 1

House lights dim

Curtain remains closed

Christian calls from off Stage Left

CHRISTIAN: Melissa!

(pause) Melissa?

(Curtain opens on …)

ACT III, Scene 1

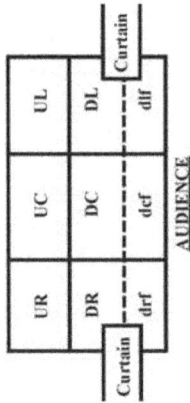

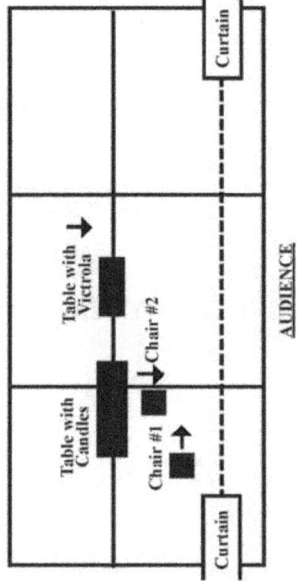

UR	UC	UL
DR	DC	DL
drf	dcf	dlf

AUDIENCE

Curtain

Curtain

Table with Victrola →

Chair #2 →

Table with Candles

Chair #1 ↑

Curtain

Curtain

AUDIENCE

ACT III, Scene 1

interior fire-gutted building
table with unlit candles
table with wind-up Victrola
chair #1
chair #2

(Lenny, flashlight on, leads Melissa from off Upper Stage Left; Melissa no longer struggles, and she holds to Lenny's guiding hand; they meander UL, UC, DC, [toward Center Stage])

CHRISTIAN: (off Stage Left) Melissa?!

LENNY: (disappointed; to Melissa) I assumed you had

more sense than to go against my express instructions, Melissa, and bring someone along.

CHRISTIAN: (off Stage Left) Melissa?!

MELISSA: If I could just let him know I'm all right.

LENNY: Better he gives up and gets out. Meandering this labyrinth, even if he had a floor plan, can be dangerous.

MELISSA: He isn't the enemy.

LENNY: Do you know how many men I've seen killed by friendly fire in my time?

(Melissa and Lenny reach Stage Center)

LENNY: I'm going to let go of you for a quick second, now. Stay put, and don't try anything dangerous, like calling out and expecting your friend to find you.

(Lenny leaves Melissa to light candles on table, revealing candles, two tables, Victrola, chair #1, chair #2)

(Lenny goes back to Melissa and motions her into chair

#1)

(Lenny diagonals behind Melissa's chair to Victrola which he winds)

LENNY: Kevin said you were best imagined twirling in a white ball gown. Quite the romantic, our Kevin. Not even Iraq took it all out of him. How beautiful his art-work, out of mere turkey bones, to have been born of so much horror.

(A waltz—"Blue Danube"—begins to play; NOTE: Lenny will let the music run down of its own accord)

(Lenny proceeds to chair #2 and sits)

LENNY: I'd offer you a little something, being flush at the moment, but Kevin told me your stand on drugs; so, I'll save us both the embarrassment of your indignant refusal.

MELISSA: (nervously) You have something to tell me.

LENNY: Only because I suspect Mr. Army Tattoo was trying to off me for what I know, before he let loose all the firepower at the Feaswell Clinic. At the time he jumped me, I figured it was a mere mugging: fellow Iraq vet fallen on hard times. I should have been made suspicious by the wad of bills stuffed in his pants, but I was too busy congratulating myself on my sudden financial windfall in having found it.

MELISSA: Now that we've your less-than-admirable motivations, can you get to the point?

LENNY: Before your boyfriend falls down an unfriendly hole, you mean?

CHRISTIAN: (faintly, from off Stage Left) Melissa?!

MELISSA: (impatiently) On the phone, you said something about Kevin, you, and some bar.

LENNY: "VN Sally's". Kevin was all gloomy, at the time, about you comatose in the Clinic. I don't think you know how much that poor screwed-up dude liked you.

(pause) Kevin spotted Captain Steven "Alien" Miller and went off the deep end. Captain Steven "Alien" Miller ring any bells with you?

MELISSA: Only in so far as a Captain Steven Miller piloted our helicopter when it went down.

LENNY: Yeah, didn't he, though? And didn't Kevin know that. So, it came as quite a surprise when Kevin saw the guy, alive and well, walk into the bar, a prostitute on each arm.

MELISSA: (indulgently) Christian and I buried Captain Miller. He was dead at the time. Believe me.

LENNY: So says you, but Kevin came barging into the toilet stall and grabbed my needle before it was even out of my arm. I offered him a clean—AIDS and all. He wasn't waiting. Damn, he needed that fix!

MELISSA: (disbelievingly) You and Kevin saw Captain Steven Miller in a bar, "VN Sally's", while I was comatose in the Feaswell Clinic?

LENNY: Kevin saw him. I was in the can shooting up.

MELISSA: No chance, I suppose, that Kevin was "clean"

of dope at the time of the sighting?

LENNY: He knew what he saw, lady. Said it would be the death of him, and it was.

MELISSA: What else, if anything?

LENNY: Kevin had met Miller in Iraq. Some Lance Corporal, name of Brent, introduced them.

(gets up and nervously paces) Lance Corporal Brent and Kevin were at the same Baghdad transit depot, awaiting reassignment. Brent had already been in-country, got a leg wound, got it fixed up, and was about to go back. He was not too excited about that and figured to buy his way out. Seems Captain Miller could, for a price, get Brent assigned behind lines. Brent suggested Kevin do the same, but Kevin was too gung-ho at the time. Of course, it only took a little while in-country, most of his unit turned by the enemy into dog meat, for Kevin, back in Baghdad for some rest and recuperation, to have a major change of viewpoint. He tracked down Brent who was suddenly no great advertisement for the good life in Baghdad.

(goes back to chair #2 and sits) Brent tells Kevin it's better fighting Iraqi insurgents in-country than doing favors for messages-from-men-in-the-moon Miller.

(pause) Ah, I see your what's-this-men-in-the-moon bullshit expression. But where do you suppose Miller got the moniker "Alien"? Miller used to brag how his "voices" saved his ass on a covert assignment into Iran, when he shouldn't have been there. Same voices saved his butt when he was caught in friendly fire upon return to Iraq. If I'd survived that many close-calls, I might believe in voices, too.

MELISSA: I met Captain Miller. My impression was that he was not some candidate for a loony bin.

LENNY: Miller's voices told him to short Iraq a few of its "Hi-GI-want-some-fun?" women.

MELISSA: Kill Iraqi prostitutes, you mean?

LENNY: Kevin decided that his killing them was no big deal. He had already, by then, seen enough dying in-country to accept Miller's sexist, watered-down version behind-lines. And Miller was interested enough to give

Kevin a trial run; seems Lance Corporal Brent had become a bit stressed out. Only took one-time, though, for Kevin, like Brent, to go all green at the gills. All a tad nastier than he'd envisioned. So, he ran back to in-country and to prisoner-of-war status in less time than it took Miller to slice and dice another Iraqi working girl.

(up again and nervously pacing) The next Kevin heard of Miller was back here, in the States, Miller gone down piloting you, Waynard, and some meteorite the Army wanted for experimental purpose. Kevin was happy as hell when he heard Miller was no more. Scared as hell, though, wasn't our boy, Kevin, when Miller resurrected at "VN Sally's"?

MELISSA: (trying to be reasonable) Forgive me if I find it far more logical, as does most everyone else, to think that Kevin was killed because of a drug deal gone sour.

LENNY: (sits in chair #2) Except it was the wrong drug of choice, wasn't it? Universal misconception: an addict is an addict is an addict. We each have our preference. Wasn't coke that kept Kevin's motor running, either. Did I tell you, my man with the Army Raider tattoo had several packets of high-quality coke in his pocket, along with all that money? What do you want to bet they'd have ended up planted on a very dead me if I'd been less the black belt in karate than I am?

MELISSA: You don't think any of this is worth telling the police?

LENNY: You have to be kidding! A tale of resurrection, witnessed by an addict, told to an addict, passed on to you, then to the police?

CHRISTIAN: (off Stage Left) Melissa?!

LENNY: (jumping to his feet and screaming) Shut the fuck up!

(apologetically to Melissa) Time for you to go. My last hit isn't giving me nearly the edge I need for more small talk.

(Lenny goes over to pinch out the candles on the table and plunges the stage back into darkness)

(Christian enters darkness from Stage Left with flashlight on)

CHRISTIAN: Damn it, Melissa, where's the bastard got you?

(Christian meanders as far as dcf, in front; curtain closes slowly behind him)

(As curtain completes its close, Christian clicks off his flashlight. A spotlight isolates Christian as....

TRANSITION to ACT III, Scene 2

(…Melissa follows Christian through the breach in the closed curtain, to dcf in front of closed curtain)

MELISSA: Christian!

(Christian and Melissa embrace)

CHRISTIAN: Thank God! What madness!

MELISSA: Let's get out of here.

CHRISTIAN: Don't think you have to ask twice.

(Melissa and Christian head dlf toward Stage Left)

(Weak-in-the-knees, Melissa staggers; Christian holds her steady)

CHRISTIAN: What'd he do to you!?

MELISSA: I'm just still light-headed from the accident.

CHRISTIAN: Which you've mentioned to John?

MELISSA: Not yet.

CHRISTIAN: You will, though.

MELISSA: Promise.

(Melissa and Christian exit Stage Left, via dlf, in front of closed curtain)

(Immediately, Melissa and Colonel Sampson, his left arm in a sling, enter dlf, from Stage Left, in front of closed curtain, and walk dlf, dcf, drf, toward Stage Right—with appropriate pauses to keep them on stage, in front of closed curtain, for duration of conversation)

MELISSA: I should have thanked you ages ago. No doubt your quick reflexes at the Clinic are the reasons I'm alive today.

COLONEL: I should have been faster. Poor Elizabeth.

MELISSA: There is one other reason for my coming to see you, though. Would it be possible for me to see Captain Miller's body?

COLONEL: (genuinely shocked) My dear Melissa, whatever for?

MELISSA: There have been rumors the Captain was spotted alive and well after the helicopter went down.

COLONEL: But you, yourself, buried him.

(recovering from surprise) Actually, Captain Miller, having no family, I've already seen to his cremation.

(Weak-in-the-knees, Melissa is unsteady on her feet, and the Colonel offers support)

COLONEL: (concerned) Are you all right?

MELISSA: It's just some vertigo left over from the crash. I'm seeing my doctor as soon as I leave here.

(Melissa and Colonel Sampson exit stage right, via drf)

(Curtain opens on....)

ACT III, Scene 2

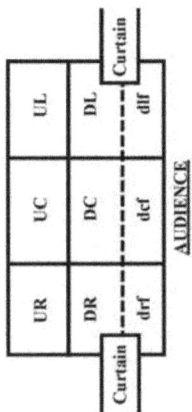

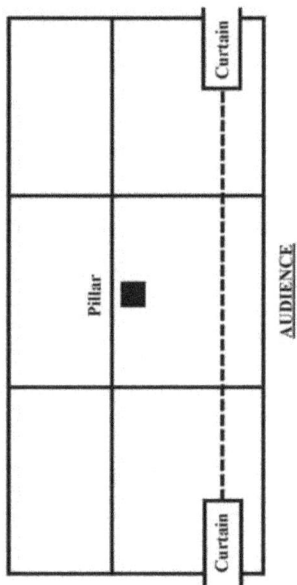

UR	UC	UL
DR	DC	DL
drf	dcf	dlf

Curtain

Curtain

AUDIENCE

Pillar

■

Curtain

Curtain

AUDIENCE

ACT III, Scene 2

underground parking garage at Feaswell Clinic
pillar, Center Stage

(Man in Ski Mask, with drawn gun, hides just to Stage Left of pillar)

(Melissa and John enter from Stage Right, en route toward Center Stage, and on a path that will take them around in front of pillar and in front of concealed Man in Ski Mask with drawn gun)

(John and Melissa pause before arriving in front of pillar)

JOHN: I'm parked over there. (nods toward Stage Left)

MELISSA: I didn't expect lunch as well as your "you're-fine-Melissa" diagnosis. Are you sure Carol won't get jealous?

JOHN: Carol was just saying we should get together and make plans for a double wedding. How about we all do that as soon as her corrective surgery is over?

MELISSA: Wasn't I surprised to discover that, among your myriad talents, plastic surgeon was one?

JOHN: The Feaswell Clinic, my dear, was built on rhino-plasties, tummy tucks, and ass hoists. Although I've since been relegated to chief administrative paper-pusher, I do like to keep my surgical skills honed.

MELISSA: It sounds as if you and Carol are moving right along in your relationship if you're talking marriage.

JOHN: As is your relationship with Christian?

MELISSA: (obviously pleased) It's coming along quite nicely, thank-you.

JOHN: By the way, I didn't exactly diagnose "You're-fine, Melissa."

MELISSA: (repentant) I know. It was more:: "Slow down a bit, Melissa."

JOHN: Your body tells you as much with these dizzy spells you've been having. Although, they don't seem serious enough to put you back in the Clinic—yet.

MELISSA: Thank God!

(John and Melissa continue to position in front of pillar and in front of Man in Ski Mask with drawn gun)

MAN IN SKI MASK: (gun aimed at John and Melissa) Surprise!

(Melissa and John turn to face Man in Ski Mask with drawn gun)

MELISSA: You!

MAN IN SKI MASK: (sarcastically) Recognize my distinguishing features, do you?

MELISSA: Back to find what Kevin told me, are you?

MAN IN SKI MASK: I had a man monitoring a tap on Kevin's phone who reported the very minute Kevin called to tell your answering machine that he hadn't yet spilled the beans but was on his way to your condo to do so. That was the good news, incoming, that provided the distraction that allowed you and Carol to make your escape. I've still the bumps from your disappearing act, by the way, which leaves me less than forgiving. So, don't aggravate me any more by being difficult.

JOHN: Which brings us to what?

MAN IN SKI MASK: I remain genuinely interested in this new knife Melissa's boyfriend is making out of Nova Scotia meteorite. Even though I, early on, figured it the booby-trap it so obviously is to catch the man who murdered his father.

MELISSA: Catch you, you mean.

MAN IN SKI MASK: Christian's father would be alive today if he hadn't come home early. I had no mandate to kill someone supplying me the means of sacrifice.

Luckily, my mentors agreed that accidents can happen.

MELISSA: And you killed and cut prostitutes in L.A. and here.

MAN IN SKI MASK: Heard about my exploits in southern climes, have you? Merely tips of the iceberg, my dear. Of significance only in that L.A. and here claimed two sacrificial weapons that aren't that easily come by.

JOHN: You're a very sick man.

MAN IN SKI MASK: And you're a very dumb one, Doctor, to insult me during whatever our time together.

JOHN: I have friends in the medical profession who …

MAN IN SKY MASK: (interrupting and genuinely irritated) Do shut up, Doctor! No mandate to kill you doesn't mean that I won't. Any more than it kept me from carving on Carol's pretty titties.

JOHN: (making a move) Bastard!

(Man in Ski Mask whacks John along side the head with

the gun; John, still conscious, but groaning, goes down)

(Melissa tardily makes her move but aborts when….)

MAN IN SKI MASK: (aims gun directly at oncoming Melissa) Do be a good girl. I don't prefer guns, but they kill just as easily as any knife does.

(to the downed John) Get up and quit blubbering like a goddamned baby!

(John struggles to his feet)

MAN IN SKI MASK: (to Melissa) I want you to listen very carefully, Melissa, so you can pass on, to the powers that be, my proposal to trade Dr. Feaswell, here, for the completed meteorite knife your boyfriend is making. And for the meteorite knife left stuck in Kevin. And, since I've been connected with the L.A. sacrifices, I want *that* knife back, too.

MELISSA: Christian might deal, but the police? I don't think so.

MAN IN SKI MASK: The police should think very carefully on the repercussions of my mailing pieces of this good Doctor to certain editors and columnists. Likewise, I can reveal some very interesting details about mutilation murders, all committed by knife, that will make several big-city police forces, here and abroad, look downright inept.

JOHN: (holding his aching head) Stark-raving lunacy!

MAN IN SKI MASK: (to Melissa) You, Melissa will wait here at least ten minutes after the Doctor and I depart.

(to John, motioning him Stage Left with a wave of the drawn gun) We'll take your car, Doctor, chancing you behind the wheel, even with your headache.

(Man in Ski Mask and John exit Stage Left)

(Curtain closes on stationary, albeit distraught Melissa as....)

TRANSITION to ACT III, Scene 3

(...Inspector Dwighton enters from Stage Right, drf, in front of closing curtain he carries a typewritten page in one hand and a stand-supported microphone in the other)

(Upon complete closure of curtain, Inspector positions the stand-supported microphone dcf, in front of the closed curtain; he stands behind the stand-supported microphone, facing the audience and gives a cursory once-over of the page he's carried in)

(Inspector clears his throat)

INSPECTOR: (taps the stand-supported microphone to be sure it's working) One...two...three...testing. Can all you hear me?

(gives another glance at page)

(to audience) I'm here, on behalf of the police department, to give you a statement, regarding the recent kidnapping of prominent local physician, John Feaswell.

Several of you have been contacted, over the past few days, by person or persons unknown, who have claimed to be the kidnapper or kidnappers and who've threatened macabre retribution and/or shocking revelations of other crimes, if the police department isn't persuaded to meet the kidnapper or kidnappers' demands. Those demands are presently under advisement and unavailable for general release. We urge you, whenever contacted, to report such incidences to our task force and refrain from any investigations on your own and/or publicizing of same. The former could be dangerous; the latter sensationalistic as regards what may just be the ravings of crackpot, or crackpots, actually unconnected to the kidnapping.

We will continue to make available to you all the particular details, as soon as they're made available to us, or as soon as they are determined to be in no way an endangerment to Doctor Feaswell's health and/or well-being.

(Inspector lifts stand-supported microphone and carries it off Stage Right, via dcf, drf, as closed curtain opens on....)

ACT III, Scene 3

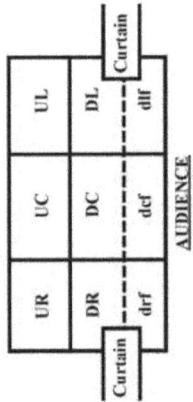

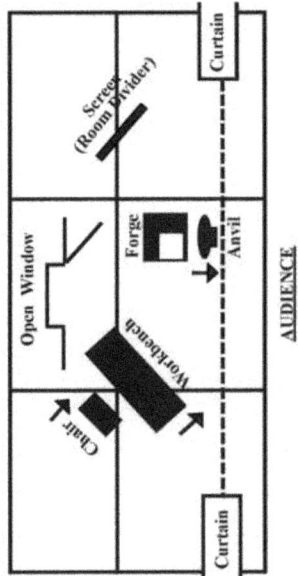

UR	UC	UL
DR	DC	DL
drf	dcf	dlf

Curtain

Curtain

AUDIENCE

Open Window

Screen (Room Divider)

Forge

Anvil

Workbench

Chair

Curtain

Curtain

AUDIENCE

ACT III, Scene 3

interior blacksmith shed on Waynard country estate
open window
forge w/glowing coals
screen that acts as room divider
anvil
workbench with scatter of papers and drawing implements
chair at workbench

(Christian, shirt off, is at anvil, hammering piece of meteorite iron-to-steel metal held by tongs)

(Melissa is seated at chair at workbench, working on de-
sign for scrimshaw knife handle)

(Carol enters from Stage Right, carrying large manila envelope which she waves to get Christian's attention; having gotten his attention, she proceeds to Melissa at workbench)

(Christian quits hammering, stuffs meteorite iron-to-steel metal into glowing coals of forge, lies tongs and hammer to one side, and crosses to join the two women at workbench)

CAROL: (indicates large manila envelope which she slides across top of workbench to Christian) A messenger just dropped this off.

(Christian unfastens the clasp of the large manila envelope and removes contents as Melissa gets up to see the papers better)

MELISSA: From our friend in the ski mask?

CHRISTIAN: (occupied with contents) Information I requested some time ago, from an unofficial source, regarding Captain Steven Miller.

MELISSA: (disappointed) Oh.

CHRISTIAN: (examining papers in hand) Rumors persist that Miller's special-forces unit was covertly ordered into Iran—and here's an interesting bit—by Colonel Greg Sampson. That name familiar? Seems the mission was to "take out" a village thought to be a supply depot for Iraqi insurgents but, only after complete wipe-out, was found not to be one.

On its way back to Iraq, Miller's group found itself under "friendly fire"—by a possibly very nervous Colonel Sampson out to dispense with any eye-witnesses to the covert into-Iran debacle. Except, Miller miraculously survived: a time bomb waiting to go off and ruin Colonel Sampson's career. A coincidence then, that all these years later, Sampson was behind Miller being assigned as pilot on the helicopter used for mete-orite recovery?

MELISSA: Colonel Sampson arranged for the helicopter to go down, so as to eliminate Miller, once and for all, all of these years later?

CHRISTIAN: That holds definite possibilities as a motive for murder, don't you think?

MELISSA: (spying something among the papers in Christian's hands) What's that?

CHRISTIAN: (shifts the papers and transfers one to the top) Says Miller contracted syphilis twice, each time from a prostitute. For which he was officially reprimanded, and….

MELISSA: (interrupting) I mean, I thought I saw a photograph. Did I?

(Christian shuffles the papers again and comes up with a file photo and cover note paper-clipped to it)

CHRISTIAN: (flipping cover note to better see the file photo beneath) Not much of a photograph.

(refers back to cover note) My source says file photos, or any photos of Miller, are hard as hen's teeth to come by.

MELISSA: And, I'll bet, not by accident!

(she takes the file photo and accompanying cover note from Christian) The clever bastard!

CHRISTIAN: (questioningly) Melissa?

(Lights Out)

TRANSITION to ACT III, Scene 4

(Curtain remains open while actors shift positions)

(Lights up on …)

ACT III, Scene 4

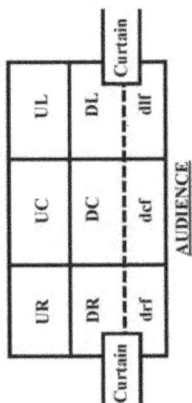

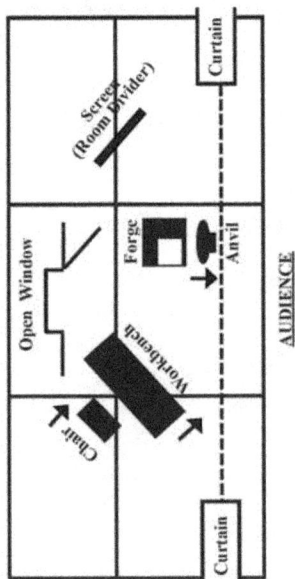

UL | UC | UR
DL | DC | DR
dlf | dcf | drf

Curtain

AUDIENCE

Curtain

Screen (Room Divider)

Open Window

Forge

Anvil

Workbench

Chair

AUDIENCE

Curtain

Curtain

ACT III, Scene 4
(Same as ACT III, Scene 3)

(Carol is positioned with gun behind screen room divider that's diagonal UL/DL)

(Melissa is seated at chair at workbench, having just attached scrimshaw hilt to finished meteorite knife blade)

(Christian, shirt on, stands behind Melissa's chair and watches Melissa wipe finished blade and hilt with chamois cloth)

(Man in Ski Mask, with gun in hand, enters through open window UC; he wears buttoned-front shirt and buttoned-crotch "501" jeans)

MELISSA: (immediately turning to Man in Ski Mask, not surprised to see him) Ah, company!

(Christian turns, too)

MELISSA: (holding up finished knife for Man in Ski Mask to see) What do you think?

(Man in Ski Masks proceeds DC and keeps gun aimed at Melissa and Christian)

(Carol, with a gun, silently emerges from behind screen, DL, and silently proceeds across DL, between forge and anvil to DC and a position that has her behind the Man in Ski Mask with gun).

MAN IN SKI MASK: (to Melissa and Christian) I think you're disturbingly unsurprised to see me early for an exchange the police haven't scheduled to happen for another three days.

CAROL: We're not surprised.

(Man in Ski Mask makes move to turn toward Carol, but she stops him with....) Please, don't turn around.

Merely hand over your gun before I blow your brains out.

(she relieves Man in Ski Mask of his gun) You might as well take off that ridiculous ski mask.

(she takes it off for him) We know you didn't go down in that helicopter crash, Captain Steven "Alien" Miller.

CHRISTIAN: Who was the sucker you got to show up for you on that meteorite-recovery assignment, Miller? Some ex-military helicopter jock, same general physical type as you, who owed you? Someone who wouldn't be missed when Captain Steven Miller officially bit the dust?

MELISSA: Kevin dead because he spotted you alive in "VN Sally's" bar? Elizabeth Howard dead because you tried to kill me because of what you thought Kevin had told me about your reappearance? Lenny Slint alive only because he was faster than the man you sent to kill him? Colonel Sampson supposed to die in the blaze of gunfire at the Clinic? Had you waited all these years to get back at him for what he tried to do to you in Iran and Iraq?

CAROL: Show him the file photo.

(Melissa retrieves the file photo from the drawer of the workbench)

MELISSA: (holding the file photo for Man in Ski Mask to see) Recognize the picture of killer / sadist / pervert / sonofabitch? This photo was hard to come by. Probably because you, and/or Colonel Sampson, did such a good job pulling anything that might have anyone noticing how the Captain Miller in the file photo wasn't the Captain Miller assigned to Elizabeth Howard for meteorite recovery and down in the helicopter?

MAN IN SKI MASK: (looking around the area) So, where are the police? It's hardly a party without them.

CHRISTIAN: We can't trust the police to handle this. They don't want to believe there are crazies like you, smarter than they are, running around loose.

MELISSA: Were you after a convenient way out, no questions asked? Too many people know your penchant for cutting and killing women? Colonel Sampson worried you'd be tracked down and open that other can of

Iran/Iraq-and-friendly-fire worms?

CHRISTIAN: Originally, we figured Colonel Sampson booby-trapped the chopper to finish off what *he*'d failed to do with friendly fire in Iraq; namely, kill you.

MAN IN SKI MASK: I told Sampson I was ready to retire and needed a way to manage it. He was happy to lend a hand. Screwing up Elizabeth Howard, in the bargain, was a bonus. She wasted a lot of meteorites with her stupid research.

CHRISTIAN: What did Sampson think when you showed your gratitude for his help by trying to have him blown away at the Clinic?

MAN IN SKI MASK: It was pure chance Sampson was there with Elizabeth Howard. Clamer was after Carol, Kevin, and Melissa. Clamer took just enough time sniffing a few lines of give-me-the-courage coke to let Kevin and Carol get away. By the time he entered Melissa's room, he was flying so high, he didn't even realize two of his quarry had flown the coop. I'm not saying Sampson dead wouldn't have solved certain problems....

CAROL: (interrupting) Enough of this killer-comes-clean bullshit! Where do you have John hidden?

MAN IN SKI MASK: The man you have come to love is somewhere safe—at least for the moment.

MELISSA: That's because if he wasn't safe, he couldn't perform the plastic surgery to give you the new identity you plan for yourself.

MAN IN SKI MASK: I beg your pardon?

CHRISTIAN: Surprised we realize, even if the police don't, that you didn't kidnap John to trade for knives, no matter how logical that might seem? You knew the police would do everything to trip you up, during any arranged exchange; maybe even succeed. Your mistake was figuring you could at least salvage this knife if you just showed up, here, early enough to claim it.

CAROL: We're not letting you have this knife. We're not letting you have your new face. We're not letting you have John.

CHRISTIAN: We're tired of playing by your rules.

(Melissa uses one arm to wipe off onto the floor, with a clatter, all that's on top of the workbench)

CAROL: (exerting pressure on the pistol in the small of Man in Ski Mask's back to push Man in Ski Mask forward) Why don't you spread out on the top of the workbench, face-up, Captain Miller? You look as if you could use a bit of rest and recuperation.

MAN IN SKI MASK: (propelled even closer to the workbench by even more pressure exerted by Carol against the gun barrel) Maybe a discussion with Inspector Dwighton is in order?

MELISSA: We think not.

CAROL: I don't want to have to tell you again to get up on the workbench, Miller.

MAN IN SKI MASK: Kill me, and Feaswell will die of thirst and starvation before you find him—if you ever find him.

CAROL: We have no intentions of killing you. This doesn't mean you won't be spilling your guts with a bullet in your leg, or in your arm, or in your shoulder.

CHRISTIAN: Come on, Miller. Up on the workbench.

(Man in Ski Mask sits on top of workbench)

(Melissa produces rope from workbench drawer and gives it to Christian)

(Christian ties Man in Ski Mask supine on the workbench, head UC, and steps back after completion)

(Melissa gets up from sitting at the workbench and turns over the finished knife to Carol in exchange for the guns).

MELISSA: (to Man in Ski Mask tied to the workbench) Now, Christian and I take a little walk, and Carol persuades you that it's to your advantage to tell her where John is. She's very concerned about John, as you might imagine. Not at all pleased as to how you'd planned to use him.

CHRISTIAN: Not to mention how you planned to kill him after he'd given you a new face.

(Christian and Melissa begin exit Stage Right)

MAN IN SKI MASK: (calling after) Think you have it all figured out?

(Melissa and Christian complete exit Stage Right as…)

(Lighting condenses to isolate Man in Ski Mask on table; Carol, with knife, moves into position on UC side of workbench, and moves chair out of the way)

(Carol places knife into light so that the light reflects from the shiny surface of the blade)

CAROL: I can't believe your voices are very pleased with you at the moment. Isn't it usually some helpless woman where you are now?

(with great fanfare, she uses the knife blade to slice off the first two buttoned buttons of Man in Ski Mask's shirt) Legally, you're already dead in a helicopter crash, Miller. You saw to that. Anything done here, by me, is done to a dead man. What kind of legal implications if someone ever cares enough to try and make the sister of a man you brutally murdered accept culpability?

(Carol cuts off the remaining buttoned buttons of Man in Ski Mask's shirt and peels the shirt flaps open over the man's bare chest)

MAN IN SKI MASK: You're bluffing.

CAROL: Am I?

MAN IN SKI MASK: I want to talk to Inspector Dwighton.

CAROL: People in hell want ice water.

MAN IN SKI MASK: (watching Carol slice off the first button of his buttoned "501" jeans' crotch). You haven't the stomach….

CAROL: I remember how it was: you with the knife in hand; I begging you not to.

(Carol slices off yet another button of Man in Ski Mask's buttoned "501" jeans' crotch)

MAN IN SKI MASK: No!

(Lights out)

MAN IN SKI MASK: (screams) Dear God, no!

(Final curtain)

(House lights on)

ABOUT THE PLAYWRIGHT

WILLIAM MALTESE was born in the Pacific North-
west. He graduated with a B.A. degree in Marketing-
Advertising and spent an honorable tour of duty in the
U.S. Army, achieving the rank of E-5.

He started his authorial career writing for the men's pulp
magazines and has since penned more than 200 books,
both fiction and nonfiction, published in over fourteen for-
eign countries. He has written every genre, including his
screen play, MOONSTONE MURDERS: THE MOVIE
SCRIPT, and a children's book, plus a number of his best-
selling women's romance/mysteries, under his pseuds
Willa Lambert" and "Anna Lambert," for houses such as
Harlequin and Carousel, included the internationally ac-
claimed Harlequin SuperRomance #2 (*Love's Emerald*

Flame), which is reprinted by the Borgo Press Imprint of Wildside Press, along with many of his other titles, new and reissued.

He encourages his fans to visit his websites:

www.williammaltese.com
www.myspace.com/williammaltese
www.myspace.com/wmaltese
www.myspace.com/flickerwarriors
www.myspace.com/draqual
www.myspace.com/maltesecandlegallery
www.mxi.myvoffice.com/williammaltese

www.ingramcontent.com/pod-product-compliance
Lightning Source LLC
LaVergne TN
LVHW091303080426
835510LV00007B/378